Myths of Enlightenment and the End of Becoming

By Roy Melvyn

D1649284

Myths of Enlightenment and the End of Becoming

By Roy Melvyn

Summa Iru Publishing

Boulder, Colorado 80020

"I had frequently read that enlightenment was like the suddenness of being struck by a bolt of lightning. In my case, it was like the cloud I was in had vaporized. I was no longer confused. There were no more edges, borders or limits. Nor were there any questions; everything was quite obvious. To this day, it continues without interruption, this totally penetrating doubt-free clarity. I spent a total of two days with Roy and I was done. I thanked him and have never seen him again."
Trevor Langford, San Francisco

"Roy's words carry the listener immediately and effortlessly along to the deepest of all recognitions, of the natural openness that we are ourselves."
Douwe Tiemersma, Netherlands, author of *Body Schema and Body Image* and *The Groundless Openness*

Contents

The way out of confusion begins with the recognition of confusion.

Then, there arises an ongoing spontaneous focus on the essence of your being. The focus is kept on this essence, on the core. Whatever else arises is neither interfered with nor engaged.

You use the ensuing insights that arise like a candle in the darkness, until the brightness is so overwhelming, that all darkness must succumb to it.

Its culmination is like the removal of cataracts, suddenly everything is clear.

Introduction

There is no blanket of concepts which one can use to cover that which you are. The viewpoint expressed on these pages reflects what I have discerned and is not set forth as a path to be followed. What path can you walk that leads to yourSelf? If it is interpreted as a path, then it has to be a path with no distance.

In some lives, there are moments that form an exception to the usual quality of perceiving. Quite often, the elementary perception of the split between 'I' and 'other' disappears.

This reveals that everything that we know is only what is perceived when it appears in consciousness. We could say that we only know movements in the consciousness. We are thus confronted with the simple fact that we have to be present first as consciousness, Conscious Presence, before any movement can take place, that consciousness is the antecedent element in every movement.

There is something in you that knows this wordlessly, although words may try to express it. Yet, if you cling to the words, my words, any words, you can never be free of them.

You think you are somebody; but you are nothing at all like that, nothing that comes and goes. What you essentially are is what you are always.

What is that?

What are you always cannot be objectified. Therefore, you are nothing perceivable.

You are always Now; you are always Here. This is your address in spacetime: NowHere.

You have no past because Now has no past. Any talk of a future for Now is only imaginary.

The world is what appears Here, what appears Now. Therefore, the world is an appearance in you. You are the Silent Background onto which it appears. You are the illuminated screen on which the images arise, move and dissolve.

Where is yesterday? When I try to locate it, it is like trying to find a dream. In fact, when I compare yesterday with my most recent dream, I find that they have a lot in common:

They both:

- Spontaneously appear, uncalled
- Feature me
- Seem to be real at the time and
- Are now gone.

Neither is Here, neither is Now. They are undeserving of further attention.

When the notion "I am somebody" vacates or is evicted from this address, it is said to be enlightenment or realization. You are free; not like a bird in the sky is free, but like the sky itself. The Realised have only realised only what is real in them. What is real in them is real in you too.

Jettison all your concepts, including concepts of what enlightenment is like, how a teacher should behave, what it means to be a student, how one ought to meditate, etc.

Remain alert and vigilant; watch yourself. Watch your thoughts, your actions, your body, everything. Take your seat in this uninvolved, impartial observation post. This watching creates space between the watching subject and the watched object. Allow the space to widen and see what happens.

Looking inwardly means seeing nothing because the inner is the subjective and it cannot be observed. When this is clear, one is released from the imprisonment within the paradox of searching for the invisible. One is free of the quagmire of a seemingly independent, self-possessed existence.

I invite you to give yourself up entirely to this discovery.

Starting Point

People take on new concepts with ease, the same as they put on clean socks. My intention here is not to provide new concepts, but to encourage you to discern that which is beyond all concepts.

Start with something small and build on it.

Something is present; yet it is not a thing. It is Presence Itself.

This Presence is experienced as a localized feeling behind the eyes, of something that's just behind the eyes, that looks out through them. It rises and sets without your approval or participation. We think it's me that is looking, but actually it isn't me, it's this Presence.

However, the intellect takes this Presence and translates it into a thing, "me". Thus, being somebody is born. The habit-energy of being somebody becomes so strong that it is even impervious to reason. That's why any intellectual understanding is insufficient.

Yet, one must begin somewhere.

When we want to know a thing, we pay attention to that thing. Likewise, if we want to know the true essence of oneself, we should pay attention to it, as object, not from identification, but from impartial observer.

See through the autobiographical narrative that postulates a self as an island, separate from life, there being some "me" which has a life, or lives a life. There are life streams and there are thought streams, originating from a single source while running in parallel.

Surrender yourself to YourSelf and see the outcome.

Dismantling the Structure

Like every expression of Consciousness, there are two components, the essence and the instrument for its expression. There is the Total Openness and the form through which the Openness expresses Itself.

The disentanglement of consciousness from a body-identity is achieved when you dismantle the structure from the center.

Suppose you have pain in the body. What witnesses that pain, said witnessing ending in the statement "I feel pain"?

First, there is the sensation of pain. Next, it is known. Then, it is labelled, pain. Last, it is expressed within a framework that uses a self-referential center: "I feel pain".

Where is an entity in any of this?

All there is is the Knowingness that knows. Objects have no knowing capability; they can't know.

Therefore, Knowing is never objective.

See this clearly. There is no one doing anything. All is happening spontaneously.

Seat in the Theater

When you look deeply into yourself, you find that you are always there, I.

I is the seat in the theatre. The theatre may be illuminated or in darkness. When lit, there are showings that are merely observable, dreams, and there are showings that are interactive, waking. To this silent, conscious, open, awareness-presence, content has been added.

I and the theatre come and go together. I never leaves the theatre in the same way as wetness never leaves water.

This Conscious Presence is what one is; there is nothing to do to be what you are.

The impediment is believing that you are a thing other than this I.

There is inexpressible openness. In It, all that is finite and limited appears and disappears. It is all a momentary appearance in the field of consciousness. Names and forms are mental formations used to establish a recognizable continuity to the incoming sensations.

You are experiencing the body and everything else as spatio-temporal phenomena. You are experiencing the mind, its images and thoughts, as temporal phenomena.

I is a fragrance; it functions as the witnessing. The entire manifest world is there because this I is present.

Self Abidance and Self Forgetting

You have forgotten yourSelf. You are conscious of a self, but are not conscious of yourSelf. The attention is everywhere but not on yourSelf. Man's inability to remember himself is his maximum security prison. A man can only escape from prison after he first realizes that he is in prison. This is the realization that can initiate further realization.

Rather than remember himSelf, man chases after happiness. In self abidance, all chasing falls away as it is unnecessary. Unfettered existence is happiness itself.

If the attention is entirely occupied with externals, one is lost in identified life, little more than a computer game. You are eating or you are showering or you are walking: you are not aware of Being, that you are, while any of these occurs. Everything is, only you are not. You are aware of everything around you, but you are not aware of your own being.

Vision of the window is very restricted when the nose is pressed up against the window. Therefore, the first step is observing from a distance. Through this, a larger viewing area is available. Self abidance creates the distance between the self and the Self. It is like the difference between looking through a keyhole and taking the door down.

Consciousness no longer blends into the environment and is now seen as distinct from it.

Self abidance is a relocation of one's attention. It is a state of consciousness in which a person is aware of their own presence and being: I am, here, now. It is prior to all the activity of the habituated machine. It is an instantaneous internal reorganization: pushing one's reflexive thoughts, emotions, and actions into the background while bringing oneSelf to the foreground.

Self abidance makes consciousness more palpable. Moments of true consciousness have been very short and are separated by long intervals of completely unconscious, mechanical working of the machine. Self abidance is a means to de-automate the usual processes which go on in the state of this automated life. In so doing, we then recognize how unconscious we really are most, if not all, of the time.

You as the Antecedent

There is an inside experiencing an outside or there is an inside experiencing an inside. That which is there, everything that there is, presents itself to the Great Space, this all-embracing Conscious Presence which results in Experiencing.

The evidence or proof of the Conscious Presence is the pre-verbal sense "I am".

Essentially, it is all a unitive closed system. The Conscious Life Energy as Subject perceives its manifestation, as objects.

Before any concept or percept appears, The Conscious Life Energy is the raw material from which it manifests itself and into which it will dissolve again.

This is what you are.

Before anything can happen, you must happen first.

Personal Worlds

Q: I don't get this idea that every world is personal. Can you explain it for me?

R: What we perceive as reality is the brain creating a panoramic scene with smells and a soundtrack. It pieces together millions of bits of information from limited, narrow ranges of light and sound waves and, with the help of the intellect, makes it into a coherent scene or story line.

In reality, the brain is just responding to electrical signals. It never really sees or hears anything. It makes us believe that we are observing what is really out there and that everyone else is seeing the same thing. In fact, neither is the case.

So you see, your world is literally of your own creation.

Consider the world of the dog vis-a-vis your world. Audio frequencies come to the dog that you can't hear, odors come that you can't smell. In the dog's world, the sounds and smells are real; in your world, they don't exist.

In fact, in humans, the variability in the sense of smell runs as high as 30%. There are things you smell that I can't and vice versa. Some are real to you yet not to me.

Every world is personal.

Q: What is hell?
R: Narcissism is hell. Self-obsession is hell.

Q: Is Advaita the highest teaching?
R: No, Aneka is the highest.
Advaita teaches not-two, only one. Yet, even this one is too many. Aneka teaches not even one.
Q: Why have I never heard of it?
R: Who is qualified to talk about the ineffable?

Q: Can you tell me why I'm so neurotic?
R: The brain longs for predictability. It makes you averse to change. Yet, you are living in an ever-changing world. How could your neuroses come as a surprise to you?
Q: Do I have to find and disregard all the changing things in the unchanging?

R; It's not about you finding all the changing things in the unchanging, but about finding the unchanging in all the changing things.

Q: What is mind?
R: The only thing you can ever know is what appears in your mind. What is called the world, including your own body, what is called thought and feeling, in short everything known by you is so only when it appears in your mind. The sum of the movements in consciousness, we call mind.

Q: Can you clearly state the primary problem and its solution?
R: The body/mind is the prison cell you have placed yourself in via identification with it. One doesn't destroy the body to overcome the identification. The same goes for the mind.
It's important to clarify that ego is not the problem. The problem is the identification with it. In dropping identification with it, the lesser is replaced by the greater, the self for the Self. Instead of a "me", the persona is viewed as "it. Little self continues or not. What does it matter?

This applies equally to the mind. Involvement or association with a "my mind" can be dropped. Then, whether it continues or not doesn't matter.
Not being somebody, not having any mind ....
isn't that why you've come all this way?
Your interest is what energizes the identifications.
Lose interest and the identifications go.

Attainment

Q: You say that virtually all practices fail. Why is that?

R: One begins a certain practice, stays with it for a number of days, weeks, months or years and then decides that it hasn't produced the desired results. So they move on to another practice that seems to hold more promise and, here again, he or she stays with it for a number of days, weeks, months or years and then decides that it hasn't produced the desired results. What we have here is the movement of no movement, going from practice to practice to practice, never seeing the root flaw.

It is like trying to change the face in the mirror by changing the mirror. It isn't the mirror that needs changing.

Q: Therefore, there is nothing that I can do?

R: Here's an idea; play with it, if you like. Don't be rigid about it. Let it reveal itself by itself.

One comes to see the polarity that exists between Subjectivity and Objectivity. When the attention is transfixed in the latter, we refer to it as identification. When fixed in the former, it is called realization or enlightenment.

How then, to create movement away from Objectivity and toward Subjectivity?

One begins by creating the smallest of gaps between one objective transfixation and the next. In the instant that I declare "I observe" while attending to phenomena, there is the briefest moment when the attending ceases. When our attention operates in an active and vigilant fashion, then thoughts and concepts do not arise, for this active attention prevents the disintegration of our Energy into these forms.

Over time, these gaps increase in duration, eventually leading to a tsunami of clarity, a steady and unwavering abidance in Subjective Being.

Q: I remember your saying that the I is the problem I don't get that; can you explain?

R: When we sit quietly, many phenomena come into our attention. We may hear the buzzing of an insect, see the redness of a rosebud and smell what appears to be pasta sauce cooking.

These are all registered in consciousness and these registrations are translated by the mind as "I hear", "I see" and "I smell". However, this is inaccurate. There is Hearing, Seeing and Smelling, all as aspects of Knowing.

In that sense, the "I hear", "I see" and "I smell" are all representations of an inauthentic-I, as opposed to the authentic-I which is the Knowing. I'll call this inauthentic-I, small i. This is the first distortion. However, that's not all.

Then, this small i looks out and sees a world separate from itself, an other-than-small-i. This is the second distortion.

It is the combination of these two distortions that results in the rampant confusion about what constitutes reality.

Q: I still don't see how to attain this state.

R: There is nothing higher to attain to.

You are already the highest, but you tells yourself otherwise. You can only know yourself by being yourself without any attempt at self-definition and self-description. Nothing happens to you; you are the center of observation of all that happens.

Turn away from intellectualism and toward pure experience. Be still, cease being anything in particular, and see whether or not my words ring true.

Ignorance

Q: Roy, lately I've been reading a lot of the ancient texts of the East. Many refer to man's ignorance as the sole impediment to enlightenment. Am I ignorant?

R: (laughing) Now, that's a loaded question!

When these texts speak of ignorance, they are referring to man's taking his beliefs to be evident truths. In that sense, if you have unverified beliefs that you're holding on to, then you're ignorant. What they make most clear is that the dissipation of this ignorance is a precondition for clarity.

I prefer to use confusion as opposed to ignorance. One is confused. Confusion is the result of taking what seems to be for what is. The Hindus refer to it as maya and the confusion is moha.

Q: Can you speak further about it?

R: Sure. It could be said that there are two views of the world, one that is perceived by Conscious and the other that is perceived by self-consciousness. The singular former is reality whereas the billions constituting the latter are confusion.

The Conscious Life Energy, its manifestation and function, and the experience of it is all there is. With clear sight, everything seen is a part of Me. Kim is a part of this Me, as is Roy, and Jack and his dog and its pups.

One may construct narratives filled with I's, you's, me's, we's and they's, but it is without real substance.

Q: If the self consciousness is the problem, how do I get rid of it?

R: It is the self consciousness itself which makes efforts to get rid of itself. So how can it be gotten rid of? If self consciousness is to go, then something else must make it happen.

The potentiality for self consciousness is the I-am thought. In its subtle form, it remains a thought whereas in its gross aspect it embraces mind, senses and body.

One must come to understand who is that "I" contained in each "my". This is the core of the investigation.

You begin at the beginning; before one conceptualizes anything, one is.

This person, this psychosomatic organism, is only an aggregate of phenomena. The body appears as a series of sensory perceptions and subsequently, concepts are formed regarding it. Yet, the senses that provide the perceptions are part of the body.

This is the paradox.

Q: Then the whole thing is outside of my control.

R: Yes, and seeing that is movement in the right direction, so to speak.

Life is the flow of individual events that sometimes intersect with this form; nothing more.

Thousands of things enter and depart from my experience without my approval. I become ill; I get well. Good news arrives, bad news arrives. I become hungry; I don't decide to become hungry.

Life doesn't need anyone's approval. In that sense, the notion of controlling life is delusional.

Mind Control and Consciousness

Q: Roy, there are many traditions that advocate the control of the mind as the path to enlightenment. What is your viewpoint in this?

R: As music is a stream of tones, mind is a stream of phenomena, of which thought is one type.

Before the effort to control, there must be the thought of control. How will the mind, which is a collection of thoughts, come under control by the thought of controlling it?

Controlling the mind doesn't take you to freedom Controlling the mind adds another link to the chains. Controlling the flow of the mind is like damming a river; all results are temporary.

Q: Well, if this is not the answer, what do you suggest?

R: Man has within himself the conscious energy to effect his transformation. However, he presently squanders the energy through his resistance to What-Is and through his energetic expenditures on attachments.

Q: How does resistance squander energy?

R: Take a very material example: if you want to stop a boulder from rolling downhill, you must exert considerable energy to stop it. You are, in effect, resisting its momentum. What-is has its own momentum; to resist it, expends energy. The desire to change What-Is into something else invariably introduces tension into the process.

In like fashion, it requires considerable energy to hold on to all the things one is usually attached to. Make a list and see for yourself.

Q: I can see that. But there are things that are undesirable.

R: Yes, that's resistance to what-is.

Q: I don't know how to get passed that. Some things are good, some things are bad.

R: See that there is no opposition between the polarities. The cyclical movement from one pole to another continues as it always has. The inherent unity in diversity is natural. Winter doesn't seek to slow the arrival of Spring.

This good-bad dichotomy is rooted in viewpoint. A cat captures a mouse; what's bad for the mouse is good for the cat.

Q: Then how can I stop thinking in terms of good and bad?

R: In one sense, you can't. Thought breeds the thinker. You assume that you create the thoughts that arrive, thus making you their thinker. But what if that's not so?

Q: Is that what you're suggesting?

R: When the Conscious Life Energy passes through the heart, one gets pumping action. When it passes through the brain, one gets thought. The brain doesn't think in the same way that the eye doesn't see. Nor does the thought "I see" see.

I'm suggesting you not take my word for anything. Check it out for yourself and reach your own conclusions.

Q: The eye doesn't see? Can you elaborate on that?

R: Let's compare two conceptual snapshots of a man.

In the first snapshot, which I'll call Mr. Yesterday, we have a man who is alive and vibrant. In the second, we have the same man, 24 hours later, laid out on a slab in a hospital, dead from a massive heart attack. I'll call him Mr. Today.

Both snapshots have eyes but only Mr. Yesterday can see. Both have ears but only Mr. Yesterday can hear. From this, one must conclude that it is not the eyes that see nor the ears that hear, but something else.

Both Mr. Yesterday and Mr. Today have brains, but only the former processes thoughts. Here again, the brain is not the active agent. Instead, it is the instrument for the activity.

In the same way, Mr. Yesterday breathes, blinks his eyes, salivates and performs hundreds of other bodily functions that Mr. Today cannot. Again, we must therefore conclude that it is not the body that operates these processes, but something else.

This "something else" is what I call the Conscious Life Energy. It is the animus to its instrument, the corpus.

Q: OK, then what is my relationship to this Conscious Life Energy?

R: Good question. The answer is that you have no relationship to it. This Conscious Life Energy is what one is.

Relationship requires self and other. One can't have a relationship with oneself.

Q: Then, when I say "I", who or what am I talking about?

R: "I" is the mind's translation of the sense of the presence of the Conscious Life Energy in the body. The "my" in "my body, my mind" emphasizes both as possessions of this "I".

The "my" in "my car" or "my wife" points to each as possessions of the named organism whose body/mind is the possession of "I".

Q: I'm confused.

R: Look at all the acts performed by the body without assigning any personal agency to them ....no one doing anything.

The instant one awakens and the instant one falls asleep occur outside of one's control. One decides to do neither.

The seeming "I" which appears is unreal. The moment the "I" is proven unreal, what is it that knows that the "I" is unreal? This knowledge within that knows the "I" is unreal, the knowledge which knows change, must itself be changeless, permanent.

Q: What I'm taking away from what you said is that it is something yet it is nothing. Can you clarify this for me?

R: One of the more difficult notions for people to embrace is that what one is is nothing perceivable. It runs counter to the brain's referential structure. You are nothing that you are conscious of. Giving this consideration causes the brain to lock up for an instant.

The only way to know this ephemerality is by its effects. Energy moving through water is called wave. Energy moving through the air is called wind. Energy moving through an inert ovum is now a living organism called Sally.

Q: I follow what you are saying and feel that I have a good intellectual understanding of it. Now what?

R: Some of you will leave here today having afforded yourselves a Masters in Intellectual Understanding. However, it is a paper crown.

What remains is for this understanding to ripen. Then its fruit drops. The ripening can be facilitated by sitting with a single question: "That which I have heard here today, is it true or not?" Don't get entwined in whether or not it conforms with your present beliefs. Begin an independent inquiry into it without any previous biases.

This is ripening.

Q: Would you say that is a summation of your view?

R: I'll restate it this way.

The only thing one can know, that one can ever know, is what presents itself in that consciousness that one essentially is.

A table or a tree exists only when it appears as a conscious perception. In other words, the only tables and the trees that one knows are appearances in consciousness.

They arise from the field of consciousness and ultimately resolve there. The appearances change instant by instant, continuously; the Seeing does not.

Looking inward, what is revealed is that one is always the silent observing of whichever perception presents itself. All these appear in consciousness, like clouds in the sky. Whether there are big clouds or small clouds, the silent observing remains itself unchanged.

All phenomena perceived, the thoughts, feelings and sensations, are nothing but movements of energy.

Every movement is in time, having its beginning, its crest and its dissolution there. Consciousness, the Experiencing that we are, is there before a movement commences, throughout its duration and after its disappearance, just as water must be there before the birth of any wave, remaining as such during its lifetime, and even after the wave has disappeared.

So-called seeking is consciousness seeking its source. There is no individual. There is only you, the total functioning as you. The total functioning is you.

The consciousness is you.

Every moment the attention is going outward toward the world. Were it redirected inward and were it to stabilize there, all your problems would dissolve.

I invite you to see for yourself.

Experiencing Consciousness

Q: To me, when I say I am conscious, it is like saying that I am not unconscious. I can say I am experiencing consciousness. Yet, somehow, that doesn't strike me as what you are talking about. Are we saying the same thing?

R: Consciousness is experience en potentia; when it touches phenomena, experience becomes actual.

In that sense, what one is is Experiencing itself. Manifestation therefore generates experience.

This Experiencing is inescapable. One may seek to alter the flavor of experience, but Experiencing remains unchanged.

It requires no doing, merely Being.

This is why we cannot talk about the experience of deep sleep.

However, there is a subtle sense of continuity; one does not cease to be.

When Roy seeks to experience himself, what he is experiences what he appears to be, that is, the subjective contacts the objective.

This obliges us to clarify: does the mind appear in the body or the body in the mind?

Surely there must be a mind to conceive the 'I-am-the-body' idea.

A body without a mind cannot be 'my body'. 'My body' is absent when the mind is at rest. It is also absent when the mind is deeply engaged in thoughts and feelings.

Saying "my body" makes one the possessor and the body is the possession. Yet, the "my" remains unresolved.

Once you realize that the body depends on the mind, and the mind on consciousness, and consciousness on awareness and not the other way round, you have aligned in the right direction.

Moving Toward Truth

Q: Roy, can you show me the Truth?

R: No, I can't.

I can show you my truth, but the two are not the same. The best I can do is to show you what is.

For example, the body does not really know anything in itself.

It is only a physical object which interacts with other physical objects. Its apparent consciousness is not really consciousness at all, but only physical interaction.

The body appears to be conscious only because its physical interactions transmit perception of external objects to our five senses.

In other words, the body is a physical instrument through which our senses know the sight, sound, smell, taste and physical feel of outside objects.

Each one of us has a unique nature, a set of operating programs that are specific to the one form. For example, as an infant, you didn't decide to dislike spinach. The dislike was hard-wired in.

A supplemental operating program kicks in at around the age of two. It is most often referred to as self-consciousness or ego. But the fact of the matter is that the brain installs, for all intents and purposes, an illusory reality revolving around an entity, "me". This subroutine is what constitutes personality and its primary function is to ensure the survival of the species.

When we see that there is no entity as such, we have moved further in the direction of the Truth.

Deconstructing Victor

Before we begin this exercise this morning, I would like to say a few things.

First, there is nothing extraordinary here. I am not extraordinary nor is what I propose, which is available to each of you. On the contrary, it is quite natural.

For those who are expecting something truly mind blowing, they should understand that it is possible, not probable.

Next, the intention of the exercise today is not for enlightenment to occur prior to your leaving here today. That's fine if it happens, but our goal is a bit less grandiose. My desire here is to merely plant a seed.

It is a seed that could lead to an intellectual understanding. Prior intellectual understanding is not a precursor for enlightenment, although it has appeared in many cases.

That seed will subsequently need to be watered, to be nourished and nurtured and played with. That's your work, so to speak.

We must understand that optimal moment-to-moment readiness, as was needed thousands of years ago out on the savannah, requires a brain that is working constantly. As such, thought is almost always in process.

Our brain is always abstracting and interpreting the world around us. Even when we know the true nature of an illusion, the insight often does not change our experience of the illusion. As far as the brain is concerned, there is no illusion; whatever it constructs, it takes to be real.

This explains why intellectual understanding by itself is insufficient and only direct apperception can provide clear sight.

Last, I want to acknowledge your coming forward Victor, and taking this initial step. OK, now let's begin.

Tell me Victor, what were you doing on this date twenty years ago?

Victor: I have no idea. I can't remember.

R: Very well. Did you exist twenty years ago?

V: Of course.

R: When you say "you existed", what is this "you" that is being referred to?

V: Me.

R: And what is that?

V: My body (pause) and my mind.

R: When you say "my body" I take that to mean the body that presents itself today. Isn't that correct?

V: Sure.

R: But that's hardly the same body that existed two decades before. Not only has the form changed, but most of its cellular structure is different.

V: I don't know what to say.

R: OK, let's examine this other aspect of "you", your mind. It too is hardly the same as it was twenty years before. Its ideas are different, as are its beliefs and opinions.

V: But the person is the same.

R: What is a person? Isn't a person an embodied personality?

V: I guess so.

R: Almost entirely a creation of heredity and society, the personality itself is the ultimate mechanism of defense, acting mostly from habit and reflex.

It is the projection of something limited, within the unlimited that one is.

All this notwithstanding, hasn't this personality likewise undergone significant alteration over those years? You can't mean to tell me that you're still playing with plastic soldiers and toy guns.

V: Of course not.

R: Good. Victor, it's not my desire to put you on the defensive. I'm only trying to show you that all these things we consider aspects of ourselves can't be such. We can't even pinpoint when this "you" began. Did "you" begin at birth, or at conception, or at the time of the planning of the conception? Do you see how slippery this is?

V: Yes, I do.

R: Now, let's return our focus on trying to identify what is common to today and to twenty years before. To do that, we must take what for some will seem to be a radical step forward.

Since we can't seem to find anything which we can call "you", can we consider the possibility that what has been referred to as "you" is not any thing, that is to say that it is not an object. Can we consider that what you really are is not perceivable?

V: (now laughing) You're carrying the ball, Roy. I'll let you run with it.

R: Fair enough. First off, you existed then and you exist now. So, existence is one piece. Second, you are conscious of existing now and were conscious of existing then. So, this consciousness is common to both.

Last, you were alive then and continue to be so today.

So let's sum it up: Existence, consciousness, aliveness.

That's what is common throughout. My term for it is Conscious Life Energy. You can call it what you like.

We have begun from a position of thinking I, as body and mind, am aware of the world. From there, the movement is toward realizing that I am this energetic presence that is aware of the body, mind and world. For most, the trickiest part is that his Conscious Life Energy has no perceivable or objective qualities.

Do you see that?

V: You know Roy, I do. But I don't know what to do with it.

R: If "I" is merely an idea with no substantive reality, what can this "I" do? What can this "I" get?

There is nothing one needs to do. What effort does water make to be wet?

That which brought you here takes you home.

V: You make it all sound quite simple.

R: It is simplicity itself. It is only the mind that complicates it.

This understanding has some far-reaching consequences. For one, it means that all searching should be suspended.

V: Why?

Because the essential nature that you are searching for is not perceivable and, as such, cannot be found. Simply be it.

V: How does someone be it?

R: What do you have to do to be what you already are? Just stop being what you aren't!

Thoroughly see that "I" is merely an idea that serves to organize and centralize all the thoughts, feelings and sensations that come to the brain. For it to be the referential center, it must be locatable and describable. As such, a continuous stream of I-am-this, I-am-this, I-am-this is established. This stream is also called ego.

However, whereas the "this's" are ever-changing, the Conscious Life Energy is constant. See that it is not this "I" that sees, that the Conscious Life Energy sees via Vincent as its instrument.

Your car is the instrument of your transportation, yet you are not your car. In the same sense, Vincent is "your" instrument, one that "you" need not identify with.

This life is a succession of physical and mental events orchestrated by a singular agency and as the ancients across all traditions have declared repeatedly: That thou art.

Inquire or Surrender

Every being has a philosophy of his own, whether he knows it or not. He may not be able to articulate it, but it is evidently operative.

Most individuals never inquire into their beliefs. To do so would be to put their beliefs at risk and their hold on sanity is so flimsy that any hypothetical dissolution of their beliefs provokes great fear. A smaller group come to gatherings like these, hoping to exchange old beliefs for new ones.

We do not gather here to trade beliefs. We are here to discern if the I can abnegate itself. If it can, let us discuss how and if it cannot, then there is no "how".

I can assure you that when you are impartial to likes and dislikes, desires and aversions, things take their own shape quite naturally. The desire to manipulate events is solid evidence of self-centricity.

When we construct an if-this, then-this notion of how realization occurs, we are structuring little more than a business transaction, an exchange. Whatever can be gained through exchange can be lost.

As humans, we seek to acquire power via acquisitions of material wealth, prestige, knowledge, etc. We seek the power that we believe goes hand in hand with enlightenment. We seek to acquire power because, deep down, we understand that our real power is miniscule.

All spiritual practices are for acquisition, performed by someone, an ego. As such, the result is egoic reinforcement.

The purpose of all practice is to discern the futility of practice. For some, it comes in a relatively short time; for others, a lifetime. Once you have discerned that the person is imaginary, what efforts, what practices can the imaginary person undertake that will result in enlightenment?

Herein lies the madness. Existence is right in front of us and we are practicing to become one with it.

The error is in viewpoint only.

Suppose I had an empty room into which I brought three chairs. Then I added three more and I counted 1,2,3,4,5,6,7. Seeing my error, do I correct it by removing one chair? Of course not, because the error is not existential, but is merely a mental miscalculation.

In your case, the miscalculation is believing that there is something you must gain and effort must be made to gain it. This is like trying to kick in an open door.

The fact of the matter is existence is already here, consciousness is already here. Stop miscalculating that you are some thing in particular and the entire universe will be at your feet.

Q: I don't believe that I can ever realize because of my karma. Can you take away my karma?

R: No, I can't, but you can. You take it away by seeing through it.

The form may have karma, this is a subject for discussion at another time. But since you are not this body, how can the karma be yours? It can only be yours if you make the body yours. Refuse to do this and the presence or absence of karma becomes moot.

Q: I want to be at peace, yet I find myself surrounded by conflict. What must I do?

R: Isn't the demand for peace the seed of conflict? As such, the more we want peace, the greater is our conflict. This world is duality; the good and the less-than-good cycle. Why not accept What-Is? That is peace.

Q: You direct us to pursue the unknown but I cannot. I am so afraid of the unknown that I am paralyzed by it. How can I break out of this?

R: You can't be afraid of what you do not know. The unknown is not the culprit. What you are afraid of is the loss of the known. The known is your anchor; its loss leaves you adrift. This is your fear.

Q: To me, the end of my ego is the same as death.

R: The disappearance of the centre of reference is not death. The continuum of consciousness, in which all phenomena rise and set, is unmoved. What dies is the trance of egocentricity, replaced by the alertness that it obscured.

Q: Who am I?

R: You ask this question because you don't know who you really are. I applaud your acknowledgement.

What you appear to be, what you are conditioned to think you are but are not, is temporal. What you call your self is some thought, emotion or sensation that you are temporarily identified with.

When you awaken in the morning, what wakes up? The sensing systems wake up. From there, "I-am-this", me, and "There is that", the world, arise.

We are constantly trying to be this or that, to achieve a particular state, to capture one kind of experience and avoid another. Sometimes we accept the unnecessary and reject the necessary. All too frequently, what we want causes us to reject what we need. What is needed is the discernment that thinking and becoming are both limited and can therefore never take us to the unlimited.

Simply be aware: "I am not the body, I am not the mind. I am simply pure awareness." As this awareness deepens, the mind's impact on you loses all force. And when the awareness is fully settled, psychological mind simply evaporates.

Q: What is my purpose in life?

R: "I am, and I know I am"; this needs no proof. Abide there and don't be distracted by questions such as "What is my purpose?" In such abidance, all questions are answered.

Q: It is very frustrating to me that you don't really provide us with any information. What you says strikes me as profound, but after I've left, I don't feel any closer to my goal.

R: The flaw in your viewpoint is that you are coming here for information. Information will only provide, at best, intellectual understanding. But that is insufficient; it is like emptying the ocean with a needle.

What is absent for you now will appear when what is present in you now is gone.

Q: I set aside three hours a day for meditation. Is that sufficient?

R: It is better to set aside the "I". Cessation of the ego occurs when the meditator turns his attention away from all other matters and focuses attention solely upon the attention itself. Constant abidance is the only so-called practice. All else is of a lesser degree.

Q: Why do you place so much emphasis on direct experience?

R: Experience is knowledge of some thing or some event gained through involvement with that thing or event. These experiences may be mental, sensory or somatic or any combination of these.

Experience is the memory of experiencing. When experiencing ends there is experience, the result. This is the goal of all seeking, results. You meditate for specific results, measured by specific experience.

Then, what is it that experiences? Consciousness experiences via its instrument of experiencing, the brain in the body. Consciousness is the Experiencing.

The brain creates a world based on the inbound sensory data. In a state of sensory deprivation, there is no world. Yet, you are and you know that you are. This is because the Knowing is not conditional on sensory data. It is self-luminous and antecedent to the world appearance.

I want you to pursue the direct experience of yourself.

Q: How can I return to my natural state?

R: The Absolute or Self is the transcendental and permanent principle of which the manifested human being is only a transient appearance emanating from the Conscious Life Energy which, itself is the objectification of Self. The Self is that by which all the states of being exist.

One's natural state is one of being, of presence and of consciousness. In this sense, you are in your natural state all the time. However, the overlaying of psychological structures onto it masks it.

Ask yourself if you are willing to forget, willing to discharge all beliefs, all opinions and every bit of seeming knowledge that you have acquired. Are you willing to return to nothing with a clean slate in hand? Imagine how much of your so called brain-space is taken up with memory and worldly knowledge.

When the 'I don't know' state is accepted, all the energy which was directed outward or inward in its search for an answer is released and is available to Knowing.

Q: Is it possible to transcend the feeling of separation?

R: Imagine that you wanted to explore the ocean floor. You would have to find a suitable vehicle, provide it with all the power it would need to operate and then you would enter inside, introduce it into its new environment and the exploration could begin.

This is no different from the operation of the Conscious Life Energy which has selected what you call your body as its vehicle for the exploration of this manifested world.

It is the mistaken equating of the Self with a body and a mind that is responsible for all the difficulty.

Seeming separation is inherent in individuality as individuality sets one apart from another, creates distinctions. In this regard, one can't end feeling separate while clinging to one's individuality. It is like soaking a stone in water to soften it.

Q: Ramana Maharshi advised the inquiry "Who am I" as the best way to realize. Do you agree?

R: Who am I to agree or disagree with Ramana? (laughing)

We read into things what we want to read. What most of you lose sight of is that Ramana was quite clear that this inquiry was of the nature of a sustained scrutiny, not something that is done for an hour a day. Too, he also made it quite clear that it was only for the ripest of souls. However, since we all believe we are above normal, seeing oneself as one such ripe soul is not too far a leap.

He also said that for those not predisposed to inquiry, surrender was the only alternative. Are you ready to make a full commitment to either?

To Swim Or To Float

A man goes to the mystic in his provincial capital and says, "Oh Great One, please help me. I believe that I am a cat. I cannot rid myself of this idea. What should I do?"

The mystic replies, "Have no fear, little one, for I will speak only the truth to you. You are neither earth, nor air, nor fire, nor water, nor ether. Know yourself as the witness, conscious of all these. You are nothing perceivable, yet all perception is because you are. In your absence, nothing is. Do you now understand, my child?"

The man answers "Yes, oh yes, Great One, what you have given to me today makes perfect sense. My understanding is established. May I now trouble you for a saucer of milk?"

Enlightenment is the eradication of the virus, the meme, the belief, I-am-this-body.

Beliefs are contagious, all the more so to those who are in need of them. Parents spread the contagion to their children who spread it outward.

People believe, "When we reach the destination, we can relax." The actuality is the reverse: if you relax, you reach the destination.

Illumination is the end of finiteness. It is not a result of resisting the virus, fighting against the virus. One doesn't fight darkness; one lights a lamp. The lamp is stillness, silence.

Where is it written that you need to be active every moment?

When the mind becomes still, one is open to a stillness that is prior to mind. In the absence of the noise that the mind makes, one discerns what one truly is.

That I am is beyond dispute. What I am is what is what we examine here.

All manifestation or actualization is an energetic movement in the stillness of Potentiality.

Once one accepts that all is consciousness, it's not much of a leap to see that "me" is the I-thought made material into a body and the world is the other-than-I thought made material.

In this manner, duality is reduced to I-am and this-is.

From the unitary Self, numerous derivative, conceptual selves arise. The identification and mesmerization with these selves is a waking-sleep. Throughout the waking-sleep and dreaming-sleep states, one pays attention only to second and third persons, and in consequence experiences cycles of happiness and unhappiness.

This ceases when the attention is fixed on the first person, Subjectivity Itself. Another name for this is Self attention or abidance.

This usually prompts the question "What is to be done?"

To renounce the world of wealth and position is a comparatively simple matter in relation to putting aside the craving to become.

All effort to control is suppression. This, too, applies to your efforts to control the pace of your enlightenment. Your efforts to bring it about only delay it.

You are sitting in the audience watching the play of life onstage. What effort do you need to make in order for the play to continue?

So, let us make clear that to speak of any attainment at some future date is to speak of postponement. The future is not yet, while the present is now. The happening of understanding need not be postponed. Simply set down all those things that preoccupy your mind, empty it, and watch understanding rush in. It is like a green pear ripening into a sweet pear. What did the pear have to do?

It all comes down to a basic difference in perspective. The doer's logic is this: if I don't swim, I'll drown. The view of the surrendered is that if I don't swim, I'll float.

Q: To no longer identify with something that I have identified with for so long is not easy.

R: I am not suggesting that it is not a challenge. Everyone around you has the same belief, that they are this body. Then surely, if they are this body, you are your body. And so confusion is perpetually reinforced.

It takes bravery to take your stand outside the crowd, to say "I am not this body, I am not this state, these states appear in me."

If the drive to identify is very strong, why not identify with the Conscious Life Energy and not restrict your identification to a singular body and mine?

Q: I have heard you use the term "most antecedent" but don't understand what you mean. Would you please explain?

R: Absence can only be discerned in one's presence. This explains why we can speak of the blankness of deep sleep, because something was present to observe it. After everything disappears, you remain.

The world being known requires an antecedent Knowing. Before anything is, I am. I am the logical presupposition or the epistemological ground of everything. My existence is proved by logic and confirmed by experience.

Q: You talk about the need for clarity. How long must it take before I become clear?

R: The future is always more alluring than the present. This is the subtle poison of "becoming". "Me", as a structure, is a work in progress, a work of becoming. One gathers constituent components, over time adds some and subtracts others. It begins at age two and usually only ends at death. This egoic drive for continuity contains its own outcome insofar as mere continuity must result in decay.

Seeing the flaw establishes the first, albeit small, crack in the foundation of narcissism.

Q: Some teachers say that listening is enough. Do you agree?

R: As the color of the room does not change unless the paint is applied, so too your "color" can only change when Understanding is applied. That explains why listening, of and by itself, is an insufficient means.

Q: What is the end of the search?

R: You go about seeking and searching from place to place, undertaking all kinds of physical and mental disciplines. The search is undertaken by what is a mere appearance with which the self has identified itself, and it is only when this fact is realized that the apperception occurs — in the absence of any individual — that what the seeker has been seeking is the seeker himself.

Q: You have not convinced me that I do not need a Master.

R: I didn't understand that that was the task laid before me.

Q: So what do you have to say?

R: What kind of a Master are you talking about: living or dead, animate or inanimate, sentient or insentient? When one approaches life with openness, Masters are everywhere.

First discriminate between what you need and what you want. Then, if you are so moved, we can revisit the question.

Q: Is the goal to be free from thoughts? Is that freedom?

R: To be free from thought is not freedom; it is incomplete freedom. To be free from thought and to be free to think, this is true freedom.

Q: How would you explain maya?

R: There is the obscuration of Essence by substance. This obscuration results in distortion, confusion. This is as close to the traditional context of maya as I will go.

Q: Can you give an example of clarity?

R: Clarity is the difference between being inside the cloud and outside it.

Q: You advise us to observe without opinion or preference. Why do you think this is the key?

R: When you observe, you let whatever happens happen. You have released the need to interfere with it.

When attention is directed towards objects and intellect, the mind is aware only of these things. That is your present state. But when you turn your attention to the Self, you become aware of It alone. It is therefore all a matter of attention. Your mind has for so long been attending to external things that it has formed an addiction to them

The process of creating conceptual entities has done you a great disservice because it has drawn your attention away from the underlying reality. In the same way that there is seeing but no seer, hearing but no hearer, there is awakening but no one awakened.

When the organism is merely observed, with the intention to understand rather than to judge, fully accepting whatever emerges, the energies that were previously allocated toward judgment are released and can now flow to facilitate further clarity.

Individuality is the awareness of the existence of "my" thoughts. Knowing who is the "I" contained in your "my" is this clarity.

Q: The traditional Advaitins say that scripture is the vehicle for realization. One reads it and one ultimately comes to understand. It seems you don't agree with that.

R: Knowing is direct experience. Everything else is the accumulation of information. One is informed, yet does not know.

Q: What is most frustrating for me is that I listen to you and I find that what you say makes sense. But you, much like Krishnamurti, avoid telling us how to do it.

R: Sadly, you have been hearing but not listening.

There is no "how". "How" suggests that there is something you can do, but there is little evidence in support of that.

There is no path to the unknown; there are only paths to the known. The purpose of any practice is to discern that practice is a dead end. The hard way to gain this discernment is to practice; the easy way is to fully accept my words.

What was Jesus' practice? There is no evidence of any. What about Buddha? Buddha made an untiring effort for six years, and he subsequently came to understand that realization is not attained by effort. So he became quiet, sat and waited. What else could he do?

I am not trying to shift your perspective from attaining through effort to attainment with no effort. I am trying to help you see that there is nothing to be attained, that at best it is a getting of the already gotten.

Taking Responsibility

You have spent your whole life in oscillation between getting away from and running toward. It is now time to stop and simply be still.

Now, just listen, without any intrusion of distracting thought.

Man finds himself separated in his mind, his life, and his body from the universal and therefore, even as he does not know himself, he is equally and even more incapable of knowing anything deemed outside. This is the result of conditioning and a conditioned mind can never understand the Totality.

It is illogical to pursue eternity while embracing temporality.

At its simplest, there is manifestation, its functioning and the perceiving of these. Another way of putting it would be to say there is life and the witnessing of life. Onto these, the human brain superimposes a psychological structure which experiences the two as "my life". This "my life", is a movement, experienced as a flow of thoughts. I am perceiving, feeling, deciding and reacting.

But it's all rooted in a distorted view of What-Is, appearing as what seems to be. This "what seems to be" is the product of mind and is rooted in an identification with an object, in this case, a psychosomatic object.

The mind must draw distinctions; in the absence of distinctions, the mind is frozen. So I will express this in mental terms: you, as the knower, are the consciousness which knows.

The knowledge is that consciousness, likewise yourself, operating; the known is also yourself, a form or movement of the same consciousness. The three are clearly indivisible though seeming to be divided.

You are the center of perception. The activities of the world and of your self-centric life all take place on the periphery. This is not easy to discern. The activity of observing is passive and subtle whereas the activities of the egoic processes are active and dynamic. As such, the latter covers up the former.

Whatever it is that is experienced as an object 'out there', can never be felt in the same way as we feel ourselves as the subject 'in here'. When one is physically 'here' and mentally elsewhere such a person is really 'there' and not 'here' at that instant of time. A person is 'here' whose mind is attending to the same phenomenal content as is the body.

The objects I and the world are perceived in the waking and dream states only and not in dreamless sleep. Dreamless sleep is thoughtless, contentless. As such, the movement of thought sources both I and the world. It appears as the first thought I-am and is then added to the second thought, in-this-world.

Q: Despite years of practice, unity consciousness has eluded me; I am still not one with everything.

R: Yes, this is most often the case. Your ego tells you that you must do something. It says this only to sustain itself. Ego equals doing.

Who taught you how to eat, how to breathe? These are actions that occur spontaneously.

The same applies here; what needs to occur will spontaneously occur when it is appropriate.

As far as being one with everything goes, there is an alternative. Just as you can traverse a circle by walking either left or right, this issue can also be traversed two ways.

The first is, as you said, being one with everything. Here's the alternative way of viewing the world: being prior to everything. While it is easy to consider the world as other, one finds it is quite difficult to consider the instrument for the viewing of the world, that is this body, as other also. Everything as other; when you thoroughly penetrate this, the clarity of it stands out like a black duck walking in the snow.

You are the subject to every object. You discern that the world is like your shadow, following you wherever you go. Yet, what harm can a shadow cause to you?

Q: Can you help me to understand my life's purpose?

R: You have a role in this manifestation and you will perform it, I have no doubt. There is no action without an instrument of action. You are the latter; all the while, the actor remains invisible.

In the meantime, observe the organism as you would observe any creature in its environment. Come to firmly know that you are neither body nor mind. Nothing more need be done.

Q: Do you also advise meditation?

R: The senses can be used passively or actively. When music is playing but we are "elsewhere", we only hear it, a passive action. But when there are no interfering thoughts, then there is listening, itself an activity. It is the application of attention to the arrival of the sense data. It is abidance as consciousness.

The same goes for seeing, which is passive whereas looking is active.

As such, I don't advise meditation; I advise abidance.

Q: I now see that the whole world is illusory. Yet, little has changed and the illusion persists.

R: According to the present illusory view, an antagonism exists between the outer world and oneself because through certain of its aspects, the outer world threatens the destruction the individual being. According to this view, the outer world is a powerful not-self, an irreducible antagonist.

As such, a change in viewpoint is clearly required.

The new viewpoint redefines outer and inner. From the phenomenal perspective, there is now no inner. All phenomena, both mental and material, are outer. Inner is subjectivity, itself non-objective.

Ultimately, enlightenment or self realization is the reconciliation of the seeming dichotomy of self and not-self. It is a process of disassembly and reassembly that occurs in an instant.

That which remains over after the disappearance of objects is It. Where there is no other, that is It. This is the perspective from the void. I am everything is the perspective from the plenum; That too is It. Stated differently, one could say that every thing is not Self, that is to say not Subjectivity. One could also say that everything is Self, Self being the source of all.

This is the paradox.

The impediment preventing this apperception is that although you accept the idea that everything is illusory, in this illusoriness you have failed to include yourself.

Q: I find surrendering to be very difficult. What can you tell me that can make it easier?

R: What makes surrender so difficult is that it doesn't offer the prospect of a soft landing. It means accepting and welcoming any and all outcomes of surrender. It is a total relinquishing of the desire to control. All these, the ego finds far too scary.

Q: How am I to know if there is any progress in my spiritual search?

R: To continue to think and speak as if you were a phenomenal object means you haven't taken in a single word I've said. If you remembered that you are the animating consciousness that gives sentience to the phenomenal objects, the question would never arise. This apperception is not gradual; the concept of progress cannot apply.

Concerns about progress are from the ego. The measure of progress is to have returned to subjectivity.

Q: Where does reincarnation fit in your overall view?

R: We know that life is temporary. Even if death is also seen to be temporary, I don't concern myself with it. My concern is solely with That which is not temporary, That which is permanent.

Q: Very well, then why do we die?

R: The Conscious Life Energy in us supplies the material by which the form is built up, maintained and renewed. Yet, at the same time, It is constantly using up the substantial form which it creates and keeps in existence. It is the food of the body and the body Its food. When the process goes on naturally, it results in decay and ultimate death. When there is an imbalance in the reciprocity, the result is disease.

Q: How can you say that there is nothing to attain?

R: Suppose you discovered a Picasso canvas in your basement. Have you suddenly attained wealth? Of course not. You were wealthy all along; you just didn't know it. The same applies here. All I am suggesting is that you take a look around yourself. Most people are so busy attaining that they have little time left to take that look around.

One word of caution: you must approach the understanding of yourself simply, without any judgments and pretensions, without any theories. That means advaita, mahayana, theosophy, zen or what have you is left at the door.

Q: I don't feel ready to undertake investigation. Is it OK if I wait?

R: How much time do you have left that you can relegate investigation to the future?

Q: I don't know.

R: Postponement perpetuates itself; there's always a better time. If you knew that the entirety of your investigation, start to finish, could be accomplished in a single day, would you postpone it?

Q: (silence)

Q: You seem to place great emphasis on acceptance. Why is that?

R: Ego is able to convert everything to its own use, even self realization. It confuses us by creating a fundamental myth: that we are solid beings. But ultimately the myth is a hoax and it is at the root of suffering. In order to make this discovery, one must see through very elaborate defenses erected by the ego to prevent the discovery of the fundamental deception which is the source of its power.

Insight arises in the absence of conflict, one such conflict being between What -Is and what one thinks ought to be. Acceptance is the resolution of the conflict. One must take responsibility for the conflicts one creates and sustains.

You can't fart and then point to the dog.

Other Books in this Series by Roy Melvyn

Seeking the End of Seeking

Disillusionment

Made in the USA
Lexington, KY
29 October 2014